LON WOODRUM

WORD BOOKS, PUBLISHER
Waco, Texas

LOVE AT YOUR DOOR

Copyright © 1977 by Word, Incorporated,
Waco, Texas 76703. All rights reserved.
No portion of this book may be reproduced in
any form without the written permission of the publisher.

ISBN 0-8499-0009-3
Library of Congress catalog card number: 77-075462
Printed in the United States of America

ACKNOWLEDGMENTS

Grateful acknowledgment is made to the publications listed below for permission to reprint poems that have previously appeared in print:

"Even in These Dying Leaves," from *Church and Home*, October, 1967, copyright © 1967 by The Board of Publication, used by permission of The United Methodist Publishing House; "Old Love Letters," from *Church and Home*, July, 1968, copyright © 1968 by The Board of Publication, used by permission of The United Methodist Publishing House; "The Heart Can Hold So Many Things," from *Church and Home*, June, 1967, copyright © 1967 by The Board of Publication, used by permission of The United Methodist Publishing House; "When Kings Went Forth," from *Church and Home*, May, 1968, copyright © 1968 by The Board of Publication, used by permission of The United Methodist Publishing House; "Incarnation," from *The Church School*, September, 1974, copyright © 1974 by Graded Press, "Man," from *The Church School*, January, 1975, copyright © 1974 by Graded Press; "Realization," from *The Church School*, March, 1973, copyright © 1973 by Graded Press; "Wherever We Wing," from *Together*, July, 1969, copyright © 1969 by The Methodist Publishing House; "My Mind," from *United Methodists Today*, March, 1974, copyright © 1974 by The United Methodist Publishing House, "Bombed Town," from *Christian Advocate*, August 5, 1971, copyright © 1971 by The United Methodist Publishing House. "Transformation," from *Christianity Today*, April 1, 1966, "We Built a Temple," from *Christianity Today*, March 4, 1966, copyright 1966 by *Christianity Today*. Used by permission. "The House" and "The Mind Knows," used by permission of *Christian Herald*. "The Spirit," "Easter Is Forever," "Elijah," and "The Rider at Dawn," from *The War Cry*, used by permission of The Salvation Army. "Thief on the Cross," from *Home Life*, April 1973, © copyright 1973 The Sunday School Board of the Southern Baptist Convention. All rights reserved. Used by permission. "Estrangement," "There Are Those," "Walking," and "Atom," from *The Columbus Dispatch*, used by permission. "Surrender," "Martin Luther," and "Song of the Magi," from *The Herald*, Asbury Theological Seminary, used by permission. "Summer Night" and "Lamps," from *Standard*, Nazarene Publishing House, used by permission. "Time Passes" and "He Sent Them Out," from *Evangel*, used by permission. "Down Goes the Basket," from *Catalyst*, May 1976, used by permission. "The Storm," "Story Teller," and "Speak, Stephen," from *Rapport*.

CONTENTS

At the Door 11
Even in These Dying Leaves 12
My Mind 13
Bombed Town 14
The Mind Knows 15
We Built a Temple 16
The Storm 17
What a World! 18
Old Love Letters 19
The Heart Can Hold So Many Things 21
Glory in a Gallows-Tree 22
The House 23
In Such Good Hands 24
Transformation 25
Evening Prayer 26
Love 27
Voice on the Wind 28
When Kings Went Forth 30
It Is Late 31
Story Teller 32
Saul of Tarsus 33
Home Flight 34
Seeker 35

There Was a Moment   36
Dark Dream   37
Lord of All Things   40
The Incarnation   41
Wherever We Wing   42
Ebb Tide   43
Atom   44
God Writes Poems   45
They Would Remember   46
Humor   47
Winter Tree   48
Prayer   49
The Butterfly   50
Surrender   51
The Spirit   52
Influence   53
Pioneer Woman   54
God Took a Cross   55
Walking   56
Martin Luther   57
Man   58
Winter Rain   59
Mankind   60
Easter Is Forever   61
The Sword   64
This Time   65
Compensation   66
Thief on the Cross   68
Sails   69

Elijah   70
Evening Meditation   72
The Rider at Dawn   73
There Are Those   76
Simon Peter   77
He Is My Brother   78
Love Can Wait   79
Speak, Stephen   80
Estrangement   81
Time Passes   82
Hail, Mary!   83
Christmas Visitor   85
He Sent Them Out   90
Resurrection   91
The Great Artist   92
Summer Night   93
Blueprints   94
Wind   95
Lamps   96
Down Goes the Basket   97
The Great House   100
Touch of Christ   102
Song of the Magi   104
Your House Will Stand   105
Had He But Been As Other Men   107
Realization   108
Assurance   109
My Clock   112

At the Door

Have we not known the hour
our hearts became aware
that love was at the door,
asking entrance there?

And some have drawn the bolt
and flung the door back wide;
while others locked the door
and let love stand outside.

And some have known tears
because they let love stay;
and houses have been bleak
because love went away.

Though one may let in pain
who lets love walk his floor,
how empty is the house
when love has left the door!

Even in These Dying Leaves

The multicolored fires of fall
upon a thousand hills confess
a burning creed: that beauty, too,
is God's along with all
things true and holy.
                       Even in
these dying leaves is loveliness.

Is not this autumn-death prophetic
that the resurrection, Spring,
will give us leaves again, and bring
us back the other things that live
and leap and fly and sing?

Did not high beauty burn in Him
who turned the cross on which He bled
into a shining glory?
                          Even his great dying
was a certain prophesying
of triumph over death, thus giving
men assurance God is God, not of the dead,
but of the living.

My Mind

My mind
is a Rembrandt
making sketches
on little scraps of time,
carelessly tossing
them into the drawers
of memory.

Bombed Town

Hieroglyphics
written in bleak dust;
the poetry of power written
for the eyes not yet gone blind.

Read these ruins,
this prophecy in rubble:
for the truth is written
in these scattered walls.
Read this shattered stone;
read, and know man's fate forever,
if his power be loosed from love.

The Mind Knows

The mind knows—even when the heart cannot
believe the door is shut.
The mind is grown up, reconciled
to bitter things; the heart a child
who sees no sense in being brave,
so cries for what it cannot have.

The mind looks on the locked-up door
and knows it will not open any more,
so bows in sad surrender, sighing;
the heart, so loath to let love go,
still hammers on the door, still crying
long and loudly: "No! No! No!"

The mind is wise, it understands;
so will the heart, but only after
lonely grief will it return to laughter.

We Built a Temple

We built a temple, beautiful and tall;
we made it stronger than a Berlin-wall.
We built an altar brighter than a star,
where we could pray, forgetting hate and war;
where we could find a refuge from the heat
of human anger in the violent street.
We heard the gentle voice of one who told
of Him who talked of peace in days of old.
Calmed were our souls till it would almost seem
that Calvary was rather like a dream.
Here we, caught in a tranquilizing trance,
could meditate in holy arrogance.
We built a church out in the suburbs, far
from where the noisy, frantic people are.
We built a ghetto out of shining stone;
walled in from man, we serve our God—alone.

The Storm

He gave his strength hour after hour
to those in need.
                He shared the power
of awesome faith which blessed
the broken, blind, and dispossessed.

At night, bone-tired, he dropped asleep
Aboard the boat that rocked upon the deep.
The black wind roared.
                Disciples, scared and pale,
cried in his ears above the gale:
"Don't you care if we die?"
                He stood,
and peace moved on the wind-whipped flood.
And afterward they must have thought:
All day we watched the works he wrought
for anguished men, then grew so scared
of wind that we forgot how much he cared!

What a World!

What a world is mirrored here
in this brief space:
the mind and feeling of the race
upon my table-top appear.
Here is reflected courage, fear,
hate, arrogance, and tender grace;
here is the fool, the seer,
the magistrate, the buccaneer,
the sot, the scribe, the cavalier;
here are the geniuses to rear
(or wreck!) a Rome or Thrace;
here man, from birth to bier,
is fashioning his strange career.

Between these book-ends: what a place!

Old Love Letters

Look not too lightly on those letters
written when love first
burned in us and words burst
from our pen like rockets fired.

We were uncommon persons
in those swift, sweet days!
We were wild poets, artists;
symphonies were in our blood,
such songs as we would
never know thereafter!
And there was silver laughter
caught in our most agonizing moments.

How could we ever be again
as ridiculously wonderful as then?

Look not too lightly on the things we said,
before the cynical façade was built,
or wild young hopes lay dead . . .
before our minds grew sharp and clever,

LOVE AT YOUR DOOR

whetted on the jagged edges
of our shattered dreams, which were,
perhaps, too beautiful to last forever.

The Heart Can Hold So Many Things

The heart can hold so many things:
wind tousling tall trees;
the sunward tilt of wings;
the sound of symphonies;
rain running silver-footed through the dust;
stars gleaming on an old church spire;
a red rose catching sunset-fire;
the ancient ocean's tireless thrust;
sails leaning on a lilac sky;
old roads that cling to river-bends;
the smell of wind from new-turned sod;
the quiet laughter of good friends;
and, oh, the silent, endless cry to God!

Glory in a Gallows-Tree

We glory in a gallows-tree.
Trees such as this
were hung with human foliage—
enough to make a mighty forest.
But only one remained
through time's long flight
while empires and their emperors
were born and buried.

We glory in a gallows-tree,
the only one on which was hung
a Man of whom it has been said:

by his death are we saved.

The House

The house was lovely
but it stood alone,
no laughter drifting
through the doors;
no footsteps sounded
on the floors;
when dark came down
no lighted windows shone.

How beautiful
some people are
who in their lonely pride
live laughterless!

Like houses, lives aren't made
for emptiness.

In Such Good Hands

We are the clay
upon the whirling wheel
beneath the fingers of the Potter, God.
These measurings of mud
are given shape and meaning by the feel
of master hands which mold
these human destinies.
These are the same bold
hands that shaped and whirled
the circling suns across
the cosmic world.

We should not shrink from hands
so sure and strong,
not even when we know the sudden knives
of pain from unexpected wrench.
                            Our lives
in such good hands could not be fashioned wrong.

We must remember in all agony:
these same brave hands once built a Calvary.

Transformation

The cross was such an ugly thing!
A shape to make the heart afraid;
a beam of death for lawless men,
a gibbet for the renegade.

The cross is such a lovely thing!
A lamp in night where people grope;
the emblem of eternal life;
the symbol of eternal hope;
the subject of a thousand songs;
the sign of truth and liberty.

The cross was such an ugly thing
until it went to Calvary.

Evening Prayer

Watching star-wheels whirling
in their cosmic courses
I wonder at the awesome forces
You possess whose order once
set fire on countless suns.
Who has an inkling of your thoughts
or attributes or powers?

Yet, watching how Your
vast creation towers
in measureless immensity,
a thought comes like an ecstasy:
You, knowing that I think of You,
think, too, of me.

Love

Love does not have to live;
it can afford to die.
It can afford to be
against a beam on Calvary.
Love does not have to live:
it only has to *give*.

Voice on the Wind

A voice on the wind of time
speaks hope from the long-ago books:
They shall beat their swords into plowshares
and their spears into pruninghooks.

Did they hear it in Waterloo's thunder;
in Gettysburg's smoke and flame?
Did they hear it in red fields of Flanders;
in Britain when deathwings came?
Did it sound when Sicily trembled,
or at death-time in Guam;
when iron shook Sinai's sand-dunes,
or in the lonely jungles of Nam?

The world heard it when mighty
cities into the dust were flung;
in the wail of the wasted children;
in the moans of the dying young.

A voice on the wind of time
speaks loudly on sea and shore:

VOICE ON THE WIND

*nation shall not lift up sword against nation,
neither shall they learn war any more.*

A voice on the wind of the world
cries long to the brutal and violent . . .
God pity the earth, the sea, and the sky
if ever that voice be silent!

When Kings Went Forth
(2 Sam. 11:1)

When kings went forth to battle,
it was Spring,
and earth from winter sleep was wakening.
Through sun-warmed dust the chariots swept;
iron ringing drowned the robin-choirs;
the children whimpered, women wept;
Through young green corn the
the war-hooves whirled;
young blood made red the tender grass.
The captains shouted and the fear-choked men
made ruin in a Spring-blessed world.

It was a time for singing when the thrill
of life was throbbing through the earth;
and kings went out to kill.

God of peace, Lord of the living, give
us faith to see the time when kings
go forth to march with Spring
and make the earth to live.

It Is Late

It is late; and we have looked far
into ourselves, and on the sweet
hope of Shiloh's Dream.
                    So many evils are
entombed in yesterday.
                    There's no retreat
into the past, our feet cannot return
to that illusioned road of man-made hells.
We are afraid; and yet we yearn
to see, beyond the mushroom smoke,
the end of war, to hear beyond
where thunder flies, the hymn of peace.
We are charged to build a Brotherhood.
Faced without hope of high estate,
O make us understand, great God,
the dream may die!
                    It is so late!

Story Teller

Speaking of raven and rain,
torn garments and grain,
broken bottles and seeds,
lightning and wind and weeds;
of sheep that went astray,
or coins a woman lost one day;
telling of wolves that kill,
or lilies burning upon a hill,
or sparrows roosting in trees . . .
talking of things like these,
speaking the simple word,
He preached the kingdom of the Lord.

We need a miracle:
the power to tell a parable!
What wonder if we could
tell tales to turn men's hearts to God!

Yet it could be in this fateful hour
we have the parables, but not the power!

Saul of Tarsus

Glorying in a gallows-beam
on which a Galilean bled,
caught in an awesome Dream,
charged with a hope immense
and faith unlimited,
girded with the ecstasy of God,
he was a new force thrusting
through a tired age,
a fierce fire from the forge of Israel,
a bugle crying in the world,
challenging the gods of hell
and earth, mightier
than legions hurled.

Behind him crosses leaped up
like flowers blooming in
a sagging old empire;
a Name was shouted and the earth
was full of fire.

Home Flight

(To a fallen Christian pilot)

God flew with you when your wings stood
a speck against infinitude
the night you thundered forth
into the frozen empty north
when curtains of infinity
swirled on the silent mystery
in darkness where you rushed
God flew with you when engines hushed
you did not fall on icy foam
but set your course for Home
across the fogless burning blue
Home with Him who flew with you.

Seeker

He looked for God;
far pilgrimage he made
to edges of the earth;
and often prayed.

He sought in classic scrolls
of men both wise and good;
in science-halls he studied
circling suns and mud.

He found God at his door
when he came home to rest,
the door he locked when he began
his futile quest.

There Was a Moment

There was a moment
which I find
caught on some corner
of my mind.

Above a lake
in frosty air
a honking gander led
his flock somewhere.

Southward they passed;
their wing-beats gone,
I heard an echo ring
across the dawn.

Still beat those wings
that southward fly;
still rings the horn that lifts
my heart into the sky.

Dark Dream

Once I dreamed a dream:
and I saw scattered through the earth
the graves of those who left their names
upon the memory of man.

Commanders whose iron-girt brigades
had made the kingdoms shake
all slept in dust unstirring;
leaders who had uttered flaming words,
or braved wide waters, leaving cities
where had been but wilderness and waste;
men who had made wheeled monsters,
or had ridden on fire into far space;
those who had made music that would sound
till time should be no more.
I saw his niche who conquered cities
in Cathay, and graves of Roman chiefs;
I paused where slept the Bard of Avon.
Fallen builders and destroyers alike
slept in their everlasting sleep.
At last I stood before the sepulchre

of him who died upon a Roman tree:
he also slept behind a Roman rock.
And I cried loud against the dark . . .
the grave had won, and death sat
pale emperor over all!

Uncounted church spires towering
above the earth were lifted lies!
Prophetic messages that moved mankind
were eloquent and senseless fables;
ages past and ages yet to come
were mindless armies marching on forever
to the gluttonous dark grave.

I woke, the dream still nagging
at my mind, and shivered in
a dying world!
              No voice of hope
broke from the cosmic void; no gentle hand
touched mine to quiet my despair.
Death mocked me silently, he who
had mocked uncounted kings and slaves
before my birth.

Then, suddenly, a bell rang:
I realized, then, dawn had come;

DARK DREAM

and somewhere in the dawn keys rattled
and a Voice rang from the heavens:
I am he that lives, I, who was dead:
behold, I am alive for evermore!

My spirit climbed like sudden fire;
my dark dream fell, a fallen cloak of lies!
With mounting rapture I remembered
Easter Day had dawned again!

Lord of All Things

God,
who flung uncounted suns
upon the measureless
black beach of night,
has made the sand
I feel warm in my hand.

My spirit,
wakened by a vision, sings:
the Lord of cosmic
mystery and might
is Lord also of all
the little things.

The Incarnation

The ultimate
was reached at last
in that strange Episode:
the Highest stooped
to touch the clod.

Love could not have
Christ less a man;
faith could not have
him less a God.

Wherever We Wing

The earthman in his thin
glittering sky-skin
climbing a column of fire
into broad black space
did not seek God in some far place,
knowing that God
stirred men on their earth-clod
into dreams of flying
through distances
awesome and terrifying;
knowing that God is not far
from any of us, wherever we wing,
to whatever star.

Ebb Tide

The crying cable
breaks the anchor's grip;
the lifting bow
stirs seaward.
          Free is the heart
from every quiet vow
made in the narrow streets
upon the land.
Fled from its bondage,
should the heart weep so
to quit the empty beach of sand?

The sea will wash away all tears;
the wind will blow
away all dreams, and drown
all echoing of any song, dismiss
remembrance of all rapture, swallow down
all tender memory.

Now, at the wind's kiss,
begins the bitter ecstasy.

Atom

Here are the elements in solar sand
that gleams upon the far black beach of God;
that glitters in Andromeda and brood
of suns that circle in Orion's band.
Infinity is caught within this thing
infinitesimal.
                Fierce power was kept
within this silent cell while ages swept
away beyond all long remembering.
In staggering minuteness here is pressed
the power of life and death.
                          The future waits
in warning stillness here behind these gates.

Here reverently let us tamper lest
the patient cosmic thunders we unlock
and make the earth an arid, icy rock.

God Writes Poems

God writes poems
but not with words
alone.
    He writes with oceans
and with flying birds;
he writes with fiery suns
and swarming stars and moons;
he leaves his penmarks
on a thousand Junes.
In wild tornadic wind,
in lilac-breath of spring,
his rhythm sweeps and swells
and lilts in gentle swing.
He whirls his magic quill
and phrase on shining phrase
is scrawled incredibly
across the scroll of space.

And while his poems glitter
on infinity's far span,
he writes his masterpiece:
the mind of Man.

They Would Remember

He rose from sleep and hushed the gale;
his shaken men sucked in their breath.
They looked on him, all stunned and pale;
they looked on water tamed and still—
how far the great calm lay!
His voice was like a cracking sail:
Where is your faith?

Long afterward, undoubtedly,
when they went out and fought
with evil forces, they would hear again
the thunder of the hurricane
about their little boat;
and they would hear again the voice
that quieted the storm;
and they, remembering, would lift
their heads in faith,
their hearts grown strangely warm!

Humor

Humor
is a pleasant
pirate boarding
my bleak ship
and sending
the sad-faced crew
scuttling into the hold.

Winter Tree

In freezing air
its branches bare
and black in winter's glow
it stands alone
in supplication on
a prayer-rug of snow,
a gaunt
dark symbol of all want,
yet paradoxically
a sign
of all the hopes that shine
out of extremity.

Arms dark
against the sky in stark
sad loneliness
it prays for Spring
to bring
a beautiful new dress.

Prayer

I am but human,
bound to err,
and full of faults
as all men are;
but though my ways
be not all good,
two things I ask of Thee:
deliver me from arrogance
and save me from
ingratitude.

The Butterfly

Young and small,
he watches while a butterfly
wing-dances on the sky.
His father, very tall,
says they must hurry.
                So,
with backward glances
he must leave, although
he cannot understand
why he who holds his hand
can't stop and look at things
which have such wonder in their wings.

Some day on other skies
he'll look at other butterflies;
but will they do the wing-ballet
as splendidly as this
one did today?

Surrender

Clay on the whirling wheel
beneath the fingers
of the Potter, God;
fashioned by the feel
of hands that mold me to his plan
I wait his work.

These awesome hands once whirled
hot suns upon a cosmic world,
and made the mystery known as man.

In hands like this do I belong;
wrought by such skill
I cannot be fashioned wrong.
In any wrench of pain
involved in shaping me,
I must remember these same hands
once built a Calvary.

The Spirit

Here must I be forever intimate,
nor ever be a stranger to your mind;
so bar me not from secret door or gate,
nor close to me the corridors that wind
into the chambers of your treasured themes.
For I must look through closets and must peer
in crypts that keep the tracings of old dreams.
So, with abandonment, make all things clear;
surrender all the keys into my hand,
nor seek to stay me in my urgent quest.
Here in this house I cannot be both Friend
and Foe, both Resident and transient Guest.
I cannot with each mood remain or move.
Here must I be at home; for I am Love.

Influence

One day
I met a true believer
on the way
who kept his faith
against great odds,
whose heart was honest
and whose life
was God's.

Remembering
that man
I walk the earth
a better Christian.

Pioneer Woman

They call me brave;
they do not know
I was not equal to the empty land;
nor know that terror rode
with me the while
the wagons rattled mile on mile
through mud and sand.
They do not know my spirit found
it took more courage far to face
security than it took to meet
the lonely world and the arrows
of an untamed race.

Less heart it took for facing
toward the unknown west
than for living under safer skies
without the tall young man who
had the wonder of a new world
shining in his eyes.

God Took a Cross

Only God could dream such dream:
taking a thing of blackest shame,
making that thing a sign supreme,
giving that thing such holy name!

Only God would dare to try
taking a thing of such unworth:
setting a cross against the sky,
certain he thus could save the earth!

Walking

Walking,
I remember how our
fingers sang together
as our feet sang on the stone.

And I remember
spring-smells floated
on the air;
and there were hills,
and high above them shone
stars till it seemed Mozart
had written something in the sky.
And I remember
you said all paths
should be wide enough
for two to walk together.

I walk alone,
remembering.

Martin Luther

Deplore his manner; call him crude;
but when your charges have been hurled
at him, remember that he
changed the world.

He opened up the ancient Book
when men were lost and blind;
he drew the shining sword of Truth
and gave it to mankind.

When nations groped in deep
and suffocating night,
he tore the darkness from men's eyes
and made them look at light.

Name all his faults;
yet will his fame
ascend forever higher.
On God's high altar
what few men have built
so great a fire!

Man

Out of the cold earth
he shapes things
that shine like fire;
he lashes lightnings
to his wheels,
climbs fire-columns into space,
pins corsages on
the desert's breast.

Dreamer and builder
and maker of mighty music,
he asks: Who am I?
Why am I here?

And his only answer
is a Name out
of unremembered time:

God.

Winter Rain

Earth, caught
in bright captivity,
bound by freezing rain,
waits for the sun to free
her from her silver chain.

Mankind

This is the pottery
of him who writes
his signature
in circling suns;
whose breath makes
immortality
out of dust;
and though the work
be greatly marred
by evil elements,
from out the ruin
omnipotence still gleams.

Easter Is Forever

Death was a pale colossus
straddling earth and seas,
mightier than the host of Caesar,
when he said:
I am the Resurrection and the Life.

He stood before the Roman chief:
"Are you a king?" the Roman asked.
I bear witness to the truth, he said.

They wounded him with brutal briars
and drove him to a gallows-hill;
they flung his back against a bandit's beam;
they put him in a borrowed hole
and locked him in with Caesar's seal
and guarded him with Caesar's sentinels.

The night fell upon his followers,
a black wolf leaping on a flock of lambs.
His enemies, wine on their wagging beards,
scoffed, laughing—"He saved others,
but himself he could not save!"

LOVE AT YOUR DOOR

Past altar-lamps of far hot suns,
an angel swept across the dawn
and lighted at the granite gate.
He dragged the stone gate from the hollow rock
and sat down on it, daring death
to try and drag it back again!

A thousand bugles were the thousand tongues
far-ringing in the land of dying men:
Christ is risen! Christ is Lord!

And Caesar's eagles shivered in the sun.

Old empire swayed; and crosses
like God's blossoms sprang from the earth,
from mainlands to the islands of the sea.

God's mighty morning kissed the world;
light-bearing legions marched
against the dynasty of death.

Down ages rang the proclamation:
I am the Resurrection and the Life!
Down ages rang the answer:
Death has no dominion over him!
And kingdoms sang the acclamation:
Christ is risen! Christ is Lord!

EASTER IS FOREVER

Death was a pale colossus
straddling earth and ocean
when he said:
*He that believes in me, though he were dead,
yet shall he live!*

And he who believes shall come,
undead and undying, to reign with him
in everlasting deathlessness.
For Easter is a promise and a prophecy.

And Easter is forever.

The Sword

He looked at Peter past the drawn iron.
"Put it up!" he said.
And Peter sheathed the bloodied sword
with wonder in his head.

Did Peter glimpse
a faint far dawn
when all men's swords would
in the scabbards rest,
undrawn?

This Time

This time I take the narrow road;
and, grappling with pride,
I trust no road-maps I have made,
for God must be my Guide.

No foe shall turn my feet this time,
nor cause me break my vow;
my heart has heard from Calvary
and it must answer now!

No friend shall breathe a word this time
my will to overthrow;
no hand shall halt me, though it be
the dearest hand I know!

This time I take the narrow road,
committing breath and blood—
the unknown road, the cross-marked road,
the shining road of God!

Compensation

I have seen the aviator's
smoky pencilings on
the unlimited blue of the sky
disintegrate until not a ragged comma
was left on the vast blue page.

I have seen the snow slip
an ermine wrap about
the shoulders of the world;
and afterward I have seen the world
wearing a tattered muddy shawl.

I have been washed on the crescendos
of a symphony, and left
when the music died, a derelict
amid the clatterings of mean
and little things.

I have walked down the road
of a magnificent dream, and wakened
to a deep and bitter grief.

COMPENSATION

I have seen the dew-splashed morning glory,
by noon, sway on its vine like
a hanged criminal.

I have seen love stride
the groaning Galilee of life;
and afterward I have seen love spiked
to the fearful cross
of empty and endless reasonings.

And now I feel:
because loveliness is so fragile,
because beauty is such a passing thing,
God gave us *memory*.

Thief on the Cross

Backed up against the beam
the robber cursed
his killers as he bled,
then turned to him who wore
the briars on his head.

Forgive them, said the Man,
for they know not what they do.
Rage in the robber cooled
and wonder in him grew.
In measure, then, he understood
why both the best and worst
were hung upon the gallows-wood.
Hope leaped in him like sudden fires;
with dying look he crowned him King
who wore the briars.

Sails

Wherever
sails stand far
on lemon-colored skies,
freed from their chains
and stuffy coves,
while old winds sing
as they romp by,
there goes that gypsy
heart of mine!

Elijah

Quick as a mountain cat,
his face like leather from the flame
of Samaritan sun; gaunt as Gilboan
crags from whence he came,
like God's wind, unannounced and alone,
he stalked the palace in his shaggy cape;
he set his face against the cringing throne,
his tongue a desert storm.
                              King Ahab shook
before his fierce forbidding shape
and the sudden judgment of his look.
Seer of Samaria, nemesis of Baal,
prophet of the angry street and sleeping wood,
he wore the troubled future in his face
and in his heart the court of God.

Flame and tormenting wind was he
in Israel unto the end;
till, beyond the retreating river,
he met God's chariot at the sudden bend
of the road.

ELIJAH

And in the alerted sky
the horse-hoofs clapped among the clouds,
with roar of wheels running
higher and higher,
and in the earth the sound of going forth
of God's wind on the wings of fire!

Evening Meditation

Who knows what God has done for us today;
what wings of mercy lifted on our way;
against what foes God's forces won
before this busy day was done?

The light of day was shining wide
to greet us when we went outside.
Ours was the music bursting from the throats
of birds—though we scarce heard their joyful notes!

Our hearts beat and we breathed, quite unaware
that heaven stalked us, Life was there!
Such good things happened—what if we were served
by silent angels unobserved?

We have not been alone upon the way:
who knows what God has done for us this day?

The Rider at Dawn

The gray rider had ridden far.

The hoofs of the pale horse
had thundered silently through Edrei
and Ramoth-Gilead and all
the battlefields of the earth.
Behind him were fallen kings and kingdoms
and a thousand prophets slept in their tombs.

Babylon was a dusty memory;
the Pharaohs were departed from
the shadows of their pyramids.

The earth was billowed with graves;
mankind slept from the river
to the ends of the world.
They lay where the glittering glaciers
stood as their tombstones;
they slept under tropic sands
and under palms and pines
on the islands of the sea;

LOVE AT YOUR DOOR

they rocked on coral couches in
the depths of seven surging oceans.

Moses had jarred enough water
from a desert rock to quench the thirst
of three million Israelis;
Joshua halted the sun in the heavens,
and held the moon over Gibeon;
Gideon had taken three hundred men
and defeated more Midianites than there
were grasshoppers on Mount Ephraim;
Samson had torn up the gates of Gaza
and stacked them on a Hebron foothill;
Daniel had troubled the lions until
they lost their hunger;
the three Hebrew men had walked unscorched
through the flaming furnace—
but all these giants had fallen before
the flash of the gray rider's sword.

The rider had ridden far and his triumphs
were beyond all numbering;
but in a Judean dawn he pulled in his pale
horse and stared at a stick on a hill;
he stared at a cross where a Man had hung;
and the cross was bone-naked
in the swiftly spreading dawnlight.

THE RIDER AT DAWN

Death, with a puzzled frown, rode on
till he drew up at a rocky cavern:
the grave-gate had been pushed away;
the tomb was like an empty open mouth
uttering a silent shout of victory!
Death swung around in his saddle,
looking back at the empty cross;
and the morning light turned
it into a thing of gold.
Death looked again at the abandoned tomb;
he shuddered in the brightening dawn,
and heard somewhere in the sky a sound
like the rattling of keys;
and a Voice came down upon him
from on high, saying:
I am he that lives, and was dead,
and, behold, I am alive for evermore:
and I have the keys of death and hell!

The gray rider, sagging in the saddle,
rode on with his head bowed;
and the pale horse limped as he went
onward into the fierce sweet dawn.

There Are Those

There are those
who walk the world
with compassion in their look;
they cannot bear
to see men chained
or hear a hungry baby cry;
they will not bow to bigotry
or compromise integrity
for either bribe or ban.

There are those
who walk this world,
driving back the darkness
as they go:
God's candles lifted
on the long night.

Simon Peter

My nets were empty;
I had fished all night
and taken naught.
The selfish sea
had let me down.

The Man rose in my boat
and at his word I cast again
and filled the nets.

Did he speak to the sea—
or to the fish?

He spoke to me.

He Is My Brother

He is my brother if he feels
he'd rather die than not be free,
and yet regrets the wheels
and wings of war,
and guns that go to sea.

He is my brother
if his heart is sad
and angry at small feet
half-clad in ragged shoes.

He is my brother
if he's troubled by
unfeelingness in men of power;
who cannot bow to biased
scrubby creed; and I,
unmindful of his color
or his clan, am bound to him.

My heart, my hand, may God
guard from dishonor
in this brotherhood.

Love Can Wait

Hate moves
with swift impatience,
bent to know
the fall of pity
and the end of faith,
feverish to see
its banners blow
in darkness over
fields of death.

But love is patient
till all time is passed;
love waits on God,
sure in its stand:
no matter what the years
may bring, at last
all ages gather
to His command.

Speak, Stephen

Speak, Stephen,
for the last time, your tongue
a hammer beating on the iron mind
of men who would not keep the Song;
beating on the barricade
of faces blind from rage.
Speak by the power of God,
the judgment from your lips
breaking on the Tarsian's code,
lashing his spirit like
a thousand whips.

Speak, Stephen,
this last time, nor flee
the stones: and when you rest
the Tarsian shall not again be free
from words you hurl into his breast;
and God's fire in your face shall be
his lamp on dark roads to the west.

Estrangement

Gray wind nags the sea;
gray sea nags the sand.
Our dreams are written in the waves,
wind-ruffled page on page.
I shout on sky and sea:
come back, come back!
Gray sea drowns your footprint;
gray wind drowns my cry.

Time Passes

Time passes
like a river flowing
or a swift wind blowing
and no one stops
its coming or its going;
none has caught
or kept it for a moment;
none will ever.
Time passes:

use it now or never!

Hail, Mary!

Hail to you who sweated
in a cattleshed in winter dark
to bring to birth the Prophet-Priest
in whose high name unholy men
and their all-holy Maker meet;
who held against your breast
a world's Savior; whose kiss upon
his infant cheek was like a tender fire;
who watched him walking barefoot
in the hot gray dust of Nazareth;
who sat with him against the wall
and heard the sparrows chirp at noon,
or with him watched the shepherds
homeward lead their flocks in purple dusk;
who taught his tongue to trace
the message of the prophets.
Hail to you who claimed no place
of power among the names your Son
set up among the stars; who did
not scold the tax-collectors
or the fishermen who took his time,

LOVE AT YOUR DOOR

or show self-pity when your house
was lonely as he took the road that rushed
to meet the gallows-beam upon the Hill;
who watched him spread-eagled
on a hoodlum's stick.
All hail to you, who when the
sword ran hot through you
and drove you to your knees
in living death, rose from your
tomb of death, as he rose
from his burial-cave;
who, not resting on your laurels,
knelt with the church to pray
in that same angel-given name
your tongue had uttered down
the sweet disturbing years.

Hail, Mary!
Daughter of the living God:
mother of the living Christ!

Christmas Visitor

The Visitor swept down
upon the sidewalk of the busy town.
He stood surrounded by the beat
of hasty footsteps in the street.
Light-trimmed trees were blazing everywhere;
and there were Santa Clauses here and there.
From overhead the speakers rang:
"Come all ye faithful—" voices sang.
Loud television hucksters cried
a message that in essence
ordered: "Hurry, buy your presents—
this is Christmastide!"

The Visitor went on his way
and frowning, slowly wagged his head.
"This Christmas seems a special day:
I wonder what it means?" he said.

He walked into a marketplace
and looked about with puzzled face.
A crowd of people shoved and rushed

LOVE AT YOUR DOOR

and squeezed and pulled and pushed.
It seemed that everyone in town
with packages was loaded down.
They stirred about like swarming bees
until the Visitor cried, "Please!"
and hurried for the nearest door.
He went into the streets once more
and said as soon as he was out:
"I wonder what it's all about?"

He went into an office, blinking
at the sound of glasses clinking.
The milling people made comments,
the most of which made little sense.
And some told loud and lurid jokes
while others grinned with glassy looks.

The Visitor went out again;
he found a church and entered in.
Before the altar candles gleamed,
but to the Visitor it seemed
the massive church was lonely;
for facing toward the altar only
thirteen people knelt to pray.

The Visitor again went on his way.

CHRISTMAS VISITOR

He asked a pair of little boys:
"Please tell me, what is Christmas for?"
And each young face a big grin wore.
"It is the time when we get toys!"

One man, who looked like human junk,
said, "It's a good time to get drunk!"
And one young cynic said, dead-pan:
"It's time off from my slave-job, man."

The festoons glittered overhead;
the Visitor in silence said:
"There must be something here amiss!
For I can't find what Christmas *is!*"

But finally he chanced to find
a gray-haired man whose face was kind
and said, "My question may seem odd, no doubt—
But what is Christmas all about?"
The other said, "Once on this earth
a Man was born in Bethlehem;
today we celebrate his birth . . .
for never was another man like him!"

"You mean he was a rich man, sir?
and gave great gifts to all the poor?

LOVE AT YOUR DOOR

He gave great feasts, this man of old,
and fed the hungry with his gold—
and that is why today we see
commemoration of his memory?"

"Oh, no. His birth was in a cattleshed;
he lived and had no pillow for his head!
He had no home beneath the skies;
and yet he opened blinded eyes;
he cured the deaf and healed the lame;
in hopeless hearts he lit a flame!
Forgiving sins which they had done,
he helped all men and wounded none.
But men were evil, they were ill:
they killed him on an outlaw's hill!"

The Visitor stared at the throng
and said, "There must be something wrong!
How can you honor him, I pray,
by all the things you do today?"

"All do not honor him this way," replied
the man, "for some know why he came and died;
they know he came to ransom men
from that great dying known as sin.
And they, redeemed by his great grace,
proclaim his Gospel to our race."

CHRISTMAS VISITOR

From overhead began to ring:
"Hark, the herald angels sing!"
The kind man said, his face aglow:
"They still remember him, you know!
And though we're fools he haunts us still;
he troubles us—and always will!
Despite our sins and wretched ways
he hounds us with his tender grace.
Despite our vulgar Christmas shame
we celebrate the day that bears his name!"

The Visitor inclined his head.
"This thing is wonderful," he said.
The other's look was like a flame!
"Ay, *Wonderful* . . . that is his Name!"

Then like a rocket thrust by fire
the Visitor rose high, and higher;
and as he wheeled in upward flight,
he heard below the music—"Holy Night!"
And as he onward, upward sped
the singing earth beneath was bright.

"*Wonderful!*" he softly said.

He Sent Them Out

He sent them out, disinherited,
despised, unknown, dispossessed.
He sent them out as strangers
in the world, east and west.
He sent them out to change the world,
these unimpressive peasants matched
against the mind of Greece.
                         He hurled
them at the iron breast of Rome.
And, having set them in array against
such odds, he saw them wrest
the world from the grip of darkness
and set the cross like fire
upon a thousand hills.
He saw them span
the years, their names like stars
burned in the history of man.

Ask not whether we believe
in Christ, but ask again
if we will share his faith in *men!*

Resurrection

Forsaken, under empty skies,
heart thrust by angry steel he dies.
Death locks his look; the tongue is still
that spoke to ages from a hill.

Big Peter stumbles in his stride
and cries a Name he has denied.
Bright tears burn hot on John's dark face,
and Mary sobs in Magdalene's embrace.

But stands an angel gleaming in the gray
dawn, shouldering the cavern-door away.
Cross standing nude in dying gloom;
dawn falling on an empty tomb.

The Great Artist

The great Artist
dips his brush
into the palette of the sun
and draws it for a thousand miles
across the canvas which we call
the sky.

At dawn he works in lavender;
at noon in green and gold
and many shades of blue;
at dusk in lilac, yellow,
and in fiery red;
then pulls his curtain
about the piece we call
Today.

Summer Night

Breeze
fingering a harp of trees;
the frogs'
symphony in bogs
bids
to drown the castanets of katydids.

The music is all merry,
except the owl's sad query,
and, from a purple hill,
the melancholy bugle of a whip-poor-will.

Blueprints

Sunset on the wheatfield;
granaries all filled;
blueprints on the table
for barns that he would build;
riches in the wheatfield,
harvests never cease!
Big barns to build . . .

Soul, take your ease!

Rich tapestries and curtains
stir in morning air;
sunrise on the wheatfield;
the day is fair.

Head among the blueprints
beside a ledger book;
bright sun on the wheatfield.

He did not look.

Wind

Last night
you screamed in anger,
shaking my house hard;
you tramped about
my flower-bed
and left it marred;
you yanked a big branch
from my maple tree
and hurled it in the yard.

This morning,
gentle as a swallow
in its flight,
you muss my hair.
You scamp! so bright
and debonair, you make
me half-forget
the tantrum of last night!

Lamps

I met a stranger in the night
  Whose lamp had ceased to shine;
I paused and let him light
  His lamp from mine.

A great wind sprang up later on
  And shook the world about;
And when the wind was gone
  My lamp was out.

But back to me the stranger came;
  His lamp still bright and fine!
He held the lovely flame
  And lighted mine!

Down Goes the Basket

A happening at midnight in Damascus:
a basket swinging on a rope,
scratching the rock wall
as it goes down.

A man riding the basket down
who will challenge Caesar's eagles;
who will give a name to innumerous men
and to high-domed cathedrals;
whose impassioned pen will inspire
a million sermons . . .

a man named Saul.

An immortal missionary hanging
on a rope held by the sweat-slippery
hands of nameless disciples of Christ.

Hard, hot hands on the rope:
hands that will write no epistles
outlasting Caesar's throne;

LOVE AT YOUR DOOR

hands that will never plant
crosses in Achai, Macedonia and Rome.
Hard, hot hands hanging to a rope:
unsung believers with a future
caught in their fists,
a world swinging in their grip . . .
a tiny task, yet incalculable
in an Administration where
a bread-loaf spreads a banquet,
a water-cup holds an ocean of mercy,
a deed well done changes
a kingdom's course.

Unsung hands steady on a rope . . .
down goes the basket bearing
its mighty burden:
the running rope a lariat looping
about continents and hemispheres
and islands of the sea:
a cable holding the church to the faith
through tormented time.

Down in the basket are books . . .
Romans, Corinthians, Galatians,
Ephesians, Colossians, Philippians . . .
down in the basket a force mightier

DOWN GOES THE BASKET

than iron-breasted legions:
down in the basket a man named Saul.

Sweaty hands steady on a rope.

The Great House

The house he built was arrogant
with haughty windows staring out
upon the world.
                      The house
was beautiful and stout;
the wood and stone were sound;
but houses stand on ground,
and treachery slept
beneath the massive walls.

The wind was like a giant's fist
against the house.
                      The flood
came roaring through the land,
a host of angry dragons
clawing at the sand.
The great house rumbled
from the shock.
The man fled from it
as it crumbled.

THE GREAT HOUSE

And he built a cabin
on an honest rock.

Touch of Christ

He touched the dumb
and dead tongues praised God's name;
he touched the blind
and cold eyes lit like flame.
He touched the angry
wind upon the deep;
the gale grew quiet
as a child asleep.
He touched five
loaves of bread
and fed five thousand
hungry men.
He touched the woman of the street
and left her spirit clean;
he touched the man whose mind was mad
and left his mind serene.
He touched the water, made it wine;
he touched the children, made them sing;
he touched the cross and made it shine;
he touched the tomb and took its sting. . . .

TOUCH OF CHRIST

Christ,
hear our cry
and touch our wounded world,
lest we die!

Song of the Magi

It gleams high in the winter gloom,
the tireless westbound Star,
that golden spark against the dark
which we have followed far.

We seek no trail in seas of sand
as down the night we ride;
the lantern-light that glows ahead
is our one certain guide.

We pray and sing while westward swing
our camels as they plod;
beyond these nights with all their dreams
we'll find the face of God!

Our hopes burn high as nights go by;
for though we follow far,
somewhere we'll look upon a King
whose Name is Morningstar!

Your House Will Stand

This is no day to build on shifting dust;
no time to build on judas sand.
The great wind tries the world.
                            The thrust
is far too great for shacks to stand.

Dig deep beneath the bog
of unbelieving years;
go down beneath the skeptic slush, down
underneath the silt of selfish tears;
go down until you hit the solid stone.

Some houses stood
in ages past when flood
and wind were loud and high;
and some will stand when all our
floods are through,
intact against the sky.

Let faith be in your building,
love beneath your wall;

LOVE AT YOUR DOOR

your house will stand
when kingdoms crack and fall.

Had He But Been As Other Men

Martha's pots
slow-simmering in the fire,
and Mary's listening face
touched by lamplight . . .

What fine hours
he spent in Lazarus' house
before he went to keep
his high appointment
on a hill.

And when his hands were
caught upon the brutal wood
there might have flashed upon
his mind the sudden thought:

Had he but been as other men,
not born to lift a fallen world,
what quiet, lovely years he might
have spent in Bethany!

Realization

Naked cross
empty tomb . . .
the realization
that self-dying
is a thrust toward
life eternal
and the understanding
that all Easters
lie forever on
the other side
of Calvaries. . . .

Assurance

I wasn't there aboard that boat
when Jesus raised his arm
and spoke to wind and water words
that quieted the storm.
But I was there when fortune's wind
blew all my dreams apart,
and Jesus hushed the hurricane
that thundered in my heart.

I didn't watch the woman touch
the Master's robe that day;
nor see the joy bloom in her face
as, healed, she went her way.
But I put out my heart to him
when life seemed bleak and vain;
I touched him in the hopeless hour
and life seemed good again.

I wasn't standing in that crowd
upon the mountainside
when Jesus spoke the Message which

the ages could not hide.
But he has spoken words to me
when life has been unkind,
and I have faced the future
with strange music in my mind.

I wasn't there upon that hill
where Jesus went to die;
I didn't see him pant in pain
or hear his lonely cry.
But nonetheless I've seen him hang
upon that brutal tree;
and deep within my heart, somehow,
I knew he died for me.

I didn't see that Easter dawn
beside that rocky tomb
when he whom they had crucified
walked from the ancient gloom;
but with a consciousness beyond
the reasoning of men,
I know he quit that place of death
and that he lives again!

I've never looked on Otherworld
beyond time's final shore,
where he has pledged that we shall live

ASSURANCE

with him for evermore;
but though the map of that high realm
be often blurred and dim,
because he's there, I'll be there, too,
sometime, somehow, with him!

My Clock

My busy clock upon its shelf
hour after hour repeats itself:
tick tock tick tock tick tock.

But once its dull vocabulary
seemed to change remarkably;
I listened in a kind of shock
and heard it say to me:

You tell your hours by my chime
and think by me you're marking time—
what if the opposite be true?
What do you do with all your days . . .
what if, in God's eternity,
I am the one who's timing *you?*

DATE DUE